Memorization in the Classroom

A handbook for teachers

Michael Rasmussen

Imagination is the source of every form of human achievement. And it's the one thing that I believe we are systematically jeopardizing in the way we educate our children and ourselves.

- Sir Ken Robinson

CONTENTS

Preface

I had just finished the 2nd year of my four-years education to become a teacher and I had decided to spend a good deal of my summer vacation to prepare me for the upcoming year, which would involve a lot of physics and chemistry. I had gotten as far as enrolling in a few online courses to expand my knowledge of astronomy, when my study was interrupted by my friend, Tony. He told me that he was exploring the world of something he called "super learning" and introduced me to the top-rated Udemy course: *Become a Super Learner* by Jonathan Levi. At first I was skeptical of this idea of accelerated learning, but my curiosity still made me dig deeper into the counterintuitive approach to learning. It made me reorganize my thinking about my subject, essentially throwing out all the lecture notes and ideas I had accumulated over the last two years.

I did not become a super learner right away, but I did apply some of the concepts in my studies, my presentations for my fellow soon-to-be-teachers and whenever I was teaching students. Eventually I stumbled across the work by the psychiatrist Carol Dweck. Dr. Dweck argued that if you were taught how the learning process works you would experience an improvement in your learning speed and comprehension – and I found this to be true.

I spent the last years as a student to improve my teaching abilities and preaching the importance of creativity and mindset. Some lectures I was attending felt boring and (in my head) unimportant, so whenever I would have to do an assignment or make a presentation, I would direct my work away from the standard theory, provided by my teachers, and instead look into the work of external sources like Tony Buzan and Sir Ken Robinson. This way of thinking led to different responses from my teachers and the other soon-to-be-teachers. Some of the words I remember being used are arrogant, brilliance, innovative and intimidating.

After graduating in the summer of 2016, I joined up with Tony and a few others to work on a project about taking learning to the next level. In the years the project was running, we would further improve our learning process by making use of the same techniques as the greatest memorization experts. Underway we had hypotheses whether students of the basic educations were able to understand and apply the memory techniques we were using. After constructing lesson plans for the subject of Memorization, we presented our ideas to teachers and principals. For the most part, we were met with skepticism, but in the end we got the chance to teach 14-year old's how to memorize a sequence of numbers. This turned out to be a huge success.

Unfortunately, we were unable to find the right business approach, so we ended up focusing on other things, while I supported myself as a substitute teacher. As a substitute teacher I would sometimes get the chance to teach my students the memory techniques and I believe that I was able to improve their learning process, after only a few lessons. In other words, I found that the concepts I was applying in my teaching could be taught directly to the students!

I still actively engage in buying books and online courses to improve my memory techniques. Some of the content in this book is the results of their hard work, other is my own personal experience. One thing is for certain, I owe most of my own success to those authors and instructors. These influencers as well as their work are listed in the bibliography at the end of this book.

Introduction

This book that you are holding in your hand is the result of me spending years of research and testing to understand my own as well as others capacity for learning and memorization. During these years, I read tons of books, watched several online courses, interacted with memory experts around the world and practiced the different memorization techniques I had encountered. In the end my findings only confirmed something that all the worlds mnemonic experts and memory champions have always known: our ability to hold and recall information is far beyond most people's expectations.

There are numerous of students who believe that their memory is bad and therefore don't engage in learning activities. This kind of thinking can sometimes be the difference between achievement and failure, whether it is about learning a new mathematical formula, win a game in

Counter Strike or do a backflip. When encountering these types of students, I always make the same statement: success always starts with having the right mindset.

I believe this statement to be true, which is why I go around saying it. The problem is that a lot of students see it as a phrase that teachers only use to be nice. In other words, the students need proof of this to be true, or else they will not believe it. For this reason, they need to see the results of being able to use their brain in ways that most adults don't. If a student with a low self-esteem can learn how to memorize words or even sequences of numbers with relatively little effort, he or she can't deny that their brain holds extraordinary potential to learn almost anything they set their mind to.

Throughout this book I will demonstrate different approaches to memorization in different subjects, including language learning. I must admit that I am not a language teacher, nor would I be qualified to call myself a polyglot at this point. Here it would be up to you, if you are a language teacher, to find the best way to apply the methods describe in this book (and especially in chapter 9) in your daily teachings. I would gladly welcome any comments you would have on this matter.

All illustrations in this book are created by me and I hope that my humble designer skills serve to give you an understanding of the concepts. You are free to show any of the images to your students to provide a visual support to any learning situation.

Chapter 1

Why Teach Memorization?

Human potential is often identified by how their skill and knowledge is used to solve tasks and to find new innovative business areas. You could say that knowledge and ingenuity have a real value and count as a parameter in our competitive society. The rapid change in tasks in a modern organization means that our skills and expertise should be changeable or agile, for example when new technology is invented, or new organization structure is formed. It makes learning more inevitable than ever before and should therefore attract the attention of all responsible leaders – including teachers.

The point is that we all should expect to be put in situations in which our approach to learning will be relevant. Because of the constant change in the world, we have to expect our job description to change a few times before we retire.

Learning how to adapt to a new skill or discipline has been one of the central abilities that companies look for, as they need this type of qualifications in their employees to survive in the long run. The learning process is what helps in this situation, the same process which is used but not taught in school.

LEARNING HOW TO LEARN

Something that stroke me when I was studying to become a teacher was how much information you will meet as a student. Still it is expected of you to be able to recall this information during tests and examinations. Looking at the way students are taught in school; it sometimes looks like the whole process of education is to prepare the students for their examination. I am not going to argue against the amount of information or the importance of some topics over others in this book. What I instead will focus on is the process of teaching and learning.

One of the things I will focus on is language learning. When I was a student in Denmark, I was taught how to speak German. One of the issues I had with that language was the classification of gender nouns. I don't remember many of the rules for gender nouns in German, but I do remember that there were specific rules and something that felt like a zillion exceptions to the rules. One of the rules that classifies a noun to be feminine is nouns ending with -ei, but somehow the word *Papagei* (parrot) is masculine and therefore an exception to this rule. A set of rules with a lot of exceptions is no guarantee that we can classify the noun correctly. In other words, we need to rely on memorization be able to remember the gender of each noun by heart. Another thing is that if I decided that I wanted to learn Spanish, which also include gender nouns, then I would not be able to use any of the rules from the German language. Teaching students how to memorize nouns is not part of the language teachers job description, so it is only natural that I was never taught this in school. But if I were, then I could apply the same principles I use to memorize gendered nouns in German to other languages, like Spanish, French and Italian.

The main purpose of education is for the students to learn, but surprisingly enough most students (and adults) are unaware of how learning actually happens. Knowing how learning happens can create more efficiency in the learning process, which will be useful for the rest of their life.

MEMORY TECHNIQUES IN SCHOOLS

By writing this book, I do not suggest that memorization is a foreign concept in any school system, as most teachers include the use of simple mnemonics in their lectures. Just think about the way you learned to memorize the alphabet. You were probably taught a song that listed the entire alphabet in chronological order form A to Z. This is a great example of a memory technique, because it creates an association between the man-made symbols (which are not easily absorbed in our brain) and a rhythm which is easier to remember. Most adults still use that rhythm when they recall the letters, but maybe not in the shape of a song. If we for example are looking for something in an index or a filing cabinet, we sometimes have to ask ourselves if P is before or after S. We know that it can be found somewhere after O, so typically we start with the letter O and then follow the rhythm O, P, Q, R, S... Typically students are not taught how mnemonics work, nor how to create their own. They are simply taught how to use some pre-made mnemonics shown to them by their teacher. This kind of thinking may be accepted by many teachers and policy makers in the context of memorization but use the same thinking in the context of math and everyone loses their mind.

The big question here is: what is the difference? Teaching students how to apply mathematical formulas to real life examples is indeed important, but the same can be said about teaching students how to create their own memorization techniques – especially because they can be applied directly to their everyday school life. Showing students pre-made mnemonics is somewhat equivalent to showing them an already solved equation. If they don't know how to do it themselves, then there is little point in showing it to them in the first place.

THE POWER OF IMAGINATION

One of the clichés that we see in the education system is the demand of making learning personal. All people are different and so are students. Some students learn best by reading, others need visual representations, and some learn best by using their bodies. The learning process is a personal process and so is memorization. If I for example tell you that I remember the number 7017 by imagining Gary Oak from Pokémon playing a guitar, you would probably label me as crazy. But this mnemonic works for me because I have a custom-made memorization system that links numbers with mental images in my mind. The memory technique I used to create this system was invented and used by the eight-times World Memory Champion, Dominic O'Brien. Few memory experts have been able to match O'Brien when it comes to titles and trophies, but what is truly fascinating is his background as a student. He describes himself as a student who had a hard time concentrating in school, had low grades and was even labeled a dyslexic. Still he manages to create the Dominic System that won him the World Memory Championship eight times. Whenever he is asked about his dyslexic he replies that he have never felt that it held him back from creating the Dominic System or winning the championships. He believes that his vivid imagination made up for his lack of academic ability.

SKILL OR PARTY TRICK?

Often memorization skills are associated with memory competitions and party tricks, like memorizing decks of cards. The truth is that there is much more to it than that. Memorization techniques can be used for fun but also as a tool to improve other skills.

Being able to hold a lot of information in your brain can be beneficial whenever we need to learn something new. In the field of cognitive psychology, memory techniques are considered to be strategies for storing new information in memory in such a way that they can be more easily retrieved. If you are a teacher, then you may at some point have come across Paget's theory of cognitive development. Piaget describe information as schemas (or building blocks of knowledge). It can be useful to think of such schemas as "units of knowledge", each representing aspects of the world, like objects or concepts. As the learner encounters new information, he or she will try to make sense of it using the already existing network of schemas in their mind. As this new information is learned it will either modify or change the existing schemas or in some cases: add new ones. For example, if you are already knowledgeable about math, then it would be much easier for you to make sense of new mathematical formulas, simply by making connections between the mathematical concepts you are already familiar with and the new formula.

Another interesting use of memory technique is to expand your working memory. In the learning process the working memory is used all the time for things like following procedures or solving math problems. The learning problems that some students have can sometimes be explained by looking at the limited working memory as the cause, because the information often slips out of their mind the moment it has entered. Working memory can be improved by implementing simple memorization strategies in the everyday life. For example, can the students be encouraged to create mental images in their mind of what they have just read or heard. Our brains are constructed to memorize images, so creating mental images can free up space in the working memory.

Chapter 2

You and Your Memory

Your memories begin forming from the day you were born and doesn't stop developing until the day you leave this world. It all starts the day you opened your eyes for the first time and had to memorize your mothers face. It then develops through your childhood as you learn how to walk and how to speak. From the point you set foot in the classroom for the first time, your memory is somewhat expected to develop at an exponential rate. When you are in school you need to memorize an insanely amount of facts, figures and methods, preparing you for the upcoming examination. Each year your learning progresses a level and you need to use the knowledge you have from the previous years to expand your knowledge in math, reading, languages and science. Learning to read requires that you can remember the alphabet and understand how they string together to form words. Math requires you to recognize patterns by remembering geometrical fact or using basic mathematical operations. You also need to remember the names of your teacher and classmates to be able to socialize. It is needless to explain further how memory is an essential function in your daily life, but do you even know how your memory works?

A NETWORK OF KNOWLEDGE

Our brain is made up of tiny little cells called neurons. These cells process and transmit information using electrochemical signals. These signals are called synapses but labeling them is not really important. What is important is to know that these synapses form networks in our brain and it is in these networks we have our knowledge. The amount of knowledge we have about a given subject is depending on how many neurons there are connected in this network. If a student is good at math, then it means that he or she have a network of connections between the mathematical formulas and real-world objects. An example would be understanding the connection between a linear function and the amount of money they must pay for a taxi fare.

A network of neurons doesn't automatically form the moment we understand something new. You should know that if you have ever struggled with something in school. You may one day in class suddenly have been able to understand what the teacher has been trying to teach you for weeks but the next day it is simply gone. Understanding something only means that the neurons have found a connection, not that we have learned it. Learning is of course built on this connection, but unless the connection stays strong, we will quickly forget again. The challenge is to make this connection stay strong enough for the brain to absorb this information or skill.

THE BRAIN IS DESIGNED TO FORGET

Like all the other parts of our body, our brain needs energy to operate. A rough estimate is that despite its relatively small size, our brain consumes about 20% of the body's energy in its resting state. The main bulk of this energy is used to transmit the signals between the neurons, so the different part of the brain is constantly updated on what is currently happening around us. One of the reasons that we forget things, is that the brain is designed to actively forget things that are not of immediate importance. The energy consumption in transmitting signals is rather high, so to keep the brain energy efficient most of the neurons in our brain are silent most of the time. The neurons are still there – ready to activate when needed.

Keeping the brain energy efficient is a huge evolutionary advantage, so it can process important information fast. The sight of a predator will immediately activate the neurons that are used to identify danger so we can quickly decide if we want to fight or flight. Any delay in recognizing the predator as a threat could be fatal. Failing to recall Pythagoras theorem in front of the whole class does not put us in any danger of dying (though it may feel like it sometimes), so the brain is not automatically going to memorize this for us. Instead it will actively try and forget the theorem to consume energy. This is why we need to convince our brain that this piece of information is important by either applying it in our everyday life or create associations to easier recall it later. The latter is often the right procedure, as it can be used to recall the information after not using it for a long time. Especially as students have no applicable use for most of the information they encounter in school.

SHORT- AND LONG-TERM MEMORY

Understanding how our memory works also includes understanding how the short-term memory and long-term memory works with each other. Basically, our senses take in information and store it temporarily in our short-term memory. If the information is deemed to be important it will be stored in the long-term memory – if not, it will quickly be forgotten. For this process to be effective, we need both the short-term and the long-term memory to function properly.

Information normally stored in the short-term memory includes remembering which groceries we need to buy or why we decided to go to the kitchen. The latter one is often a problem for many and can be a sign of a weakened short-term memory.

In the long-term memory we strive to store information which we find important (even if we sometimes have to convince our brain that it is the case). This includes important information from school or books, pin-codes and names. Studies from 1956 shows that the adult brain typically can store five to nine pieces of information in the short-term memory, without the use of any memorization techniques. This is known as Miller's Law or the Magical Number Seven (seven items, plus/minus two). The long-term memory in comparison has unlimited storage capacity.

In the long-term memory we have taken the information from the short-term memory and made sure that we can use it later. A lot of learning happening in schools are only stored in the short-term memory and is therefore forgotten after a few hours has passed. This happens because, even though the students understand the concept in the classroom, they have not converted it to the long-term memory so after a few hours of not working with the subject, the memory will be forgotten. To convert the information from the short-term memory to the long-term memory we can use two approaches: rote learning and association.

ROTE LEARNING

Rote learning (learning by repetition) is the one most used as it is the logical choice for many. The procedure typically involves repeating the same information or method over and over again to make it stick in our memory. Some examples of rote learning include repeatedly writing vocabulary words, reciting facts, or constantly practice math and spelling. These are all examples of how rote learning is continually used in schools to promote learning, though one of the problems with rote learning is that the information only is stored in the short-term memory.

Consistent repetition can temporarily store the information in the long-term memory, but it doesn't mean that we will remember it forever. The only way to keep the information in our long-term memory is to use the information consistently. The more we recall the information from our memory, the more likely it is that the information will stick in our brain. However, in most education systems we have no immediate use for the information after we pass the test so even if we need the information a few years later we will find that the information is no longer stored in our memory.

Another problem with rote learning is that is doesn't give us a deep understanding of the subject. Rote learning only helps us remember the information, but to truly learn something we need to be able to connect it with a past experience and understand how it works in context with the world around us. If we don't understand this context, then the information we memorize is of little importance and directly useless in further learning. Part of the reason why some students forget simple formulas and rules is because they lack the past experience needed to solve the equation mathematically.

LEARNING BY ASSOCIATION

Luckily for us, there are alternatives to rote learning. While rote learning typically appeals to the short-term memory, we can store information in the long-term memory by associating the information with something we are already familiar with. The best way to learn something new is to connect it to past knowledge or a personal experience we have had. Making a connection between the new information and something we already know, creates a context with the information and makes it much more memorable. For example, you may have been taught the alphabet by singing the song. Do you still remember it? You probably do and the reason for that is that your teacher taught you a mnemonic. Creating mnemonics is a useful tactic for learning because we create new memories in the form of stories, songs, images and muscle memories. Such memories are powerful because they are easier to remember, even if the information contained is simply a string of letters or numbers.

In this book I will of course move beyond the this. Using the methods describing in this book or simply being aware of their existing can kickstart the learning process for a lot of your students, your kids or even yourself as a learning.

Chapter 3

The Three Stages of Memorization

Understanding how the memory works is a great way to improve the memorization process, but before we can dive into the good stuff, you need to understand the three stages in the memorization process. From encountering the information to later being able to recall it, the whole process can be categorized into three stages:

- Encoding
- Storage
- Retrieval

Understanding the flow as well as your role as a teacher in each stage can sometimes be the backbone in your student's memorization process.

ENCODING

The encoding process is the first stage in memorization. As the name suggest this is the stage where our brain is creating the memories from the impressions, we get though our senses. In this stage our memory is fragile because the impressions have not yet been converted into memories, so in this stage we can easily lose the memories again. We receive the impressions through our senses, primarily through vision and acoustic. This is also the stage in which we notice patterns in the information. The encoding process is used in both short-term and long-term memory creation, but it is most important in the short-term memory state, because the encoding is only superficial which is why the information is easily forgotten.

An example could be if you are in the process of dialing a phone number. Seeing the phone number on a website or flyer gives you a visual encoding, so you basically have an instantaneous memory of what the phone number "looks like". If you are in the habit of reading the number out loud, you are using acoustic encoding to remember what the phone number "sounds like". If you see patterns in the phone number, like the last three digits are the same number, or part of the number is your birthday, then you use semantic encoding to add meaning to it. All three of these encoding methods helps you to store the phone number in the short-term memory.

In the classroom this stage would be equivalent to you using different visual representations, like diagrams, images or movies while explaining the concept and relating it to something the students understand. For long-term memory creation, we need the students to manually convert the encoded information to meaningful memories which can be stored in their long-term memory.

STORAGE

The storage process is the second stage of memorization and is the stage that converts the encoded information to the long-term memory. This stage is often skipped in rote learning, as it usually is about repeating the encoding process again and again, and later try to recall the information. Using the memorization techniques taught in the following chapters, we can convert the information we need to remember to mental images. Because of our brains ability to easier remember images than text or numbers, we can use these mental images as place holders.

Earlier I mentioned how I use a mental image of Gary Oak playing guitar to remember the number 7017. In the encoding process, we would probably encode the number using vision, acoustic and semantic (notice that it starts and ends with seven) which would store the number temporarily in our short-term memory. This number is stored in my own long-term memory, because I have used the Dominic System to convert the number to the mental image which is easier for me to remember. This method will be described in dept in chapter 8.

This stage is the only stage in which us teachers are not directly involved, given that the students has been taught how to create their own mental images. Memorization and association are always personal which the example above demonstrates. The Dominic System as a memorization method can be used by everybody, but so far, I have not encountered someone besides me who have used this specific mental image in their own personal Dominic

System.

RETRIEVAL

The retrieval process is the final stage in memorization and it is the stage in which we retrieve the stored information. It is directly linked with the memorization method we used to store the information. In the example from before, I converted the number 7017 to the mental image, so the way I recall the number 7017 is by finding the mental image of Gary Oak playing guitar in my mind and then convert it back to the number 7017.

Using methods to organize the memories can be helpful in this stage, as it enhances our ability to find the right memory. A popular method to organize memories if the Memory Palace, which will be introduced in chapter 5.

The retrieval stage can be used as a tool to evaluate all three stages in the memorization process. Failure to retrieve the information can be a sign that something has gone wrong in either the encoding or storage stage, or simply that the memory system we use has flaws and needs to be redone. Your job as a teacher would of course be to use your knowledge of the students to evaluate whether the encoding process should be improved or if the problem lies with the student's memorization method. It is not uncommon to forget sometimes but if it happens too often, we need to find the reason.

Chapter 4

The Power of Imagination

When I was a kid, I loved reading books. Whenever I found a book that really hooked me, I would sink into it without paying much attention to my surroundings. Afterwards I would sometimes sit back and think back on the story I had just read, playing the scenes in my head, like I had just watched a movie. Whenever I tried to explain this to others, I was often told that I might have too much of an imagination. That was true and I knew that – I just couldn't help it.

The reason why I was able to remember this much was because I always created mental images that rolled like a filmstrip in my head. After watching the first Harry Potter movie I read all the books released at that point and played the scenes inside my head by creating mental images based on the characters from the movies (it really bugged me that the movies never introduced Peeves, because he was hard to imagine). Whenever new characters were introduced, I imagined what they might look like based on the description in the books.

All memory involves linking one piece of information to another. More specifically, remembering anything new involves associating that piece of information with something we know already. For most people who have not been trained in memory techniques, this process is purely subconscious (like me in my childhood). Sometimes, our subconscious mind makes strong associations and sometimes weak ones. When the associations are strong, we find that we can remember the information easily.

MNEMONICS

The idea of using mnemonics to memorize information origins from the old Greece. Even the word mnemonics comes from the Greek goddess of memory: Mnemosyne. Politicians and senators in the old Greece and Roman empire would use the techniques that you are about to learn to impress each other and the public with their apparently superhuman ability to recall information. The technique they used was simple but effective. What they did was to take the information that they had to remember and then use their imagination to convert it into a mental image. Why? Because images are often easier to remember than words and numbers.

For this reason, it can be very beneficial to learn how to transform information into something we can relate to, be it a mental image, a rhyme or a rhythm. As we grow up, we are often discoursed from using our imagination in this way, simply because it is "childish". Funny thing is that children naturally have a great foundation to memorize - mainly because their memorization process has not yet been discouraged. You may already know this if you have been playing a "flip the cards" memory game with a child. Somehow, they are very good at remembering the images on the cards often better than adults.

VISUALIZATION

The ability to visualize something is one of the most powerful tools in memorization. Our brain is designed to think in pictures, so we tend to remember pictures better than words. The more detailed and outstanding the picture appears in our minds, the stronger our memory of it will be. The reason why most people forget easily is because they try to remember words. Words (and numbers for that matter) only appeared recently in the human evolution, so our brains are not designed to memorize such things. Our brains are more concerned about memorizing the appearance of a predator or the characteristics of a poisonous plant than so-called useless information of who discovered electromagnetism. Still there are ways to remember such things. The secret is to convert the information to mental images that easier stick to our brain. Later when we need the information, we can recall the mental images and translate it into the information we need.

CREATING MENTAL IMAGES

When we create mental images to memorize information, it is important to use images that comes natural to us. Different people imagine different things, so the mental images we use are highly different. Think about the way you would remember a dog.

The mental image for dog could be:

- **Personal,** a dog you had as a child.
- **Stereotypical,** a typical type of dog, like the German Shepherd.
- **Animated,** a dog from a game like Dogmeat from Fallout 3.
- **Comic-style,** a comical representation of a dog, like Goofy.
- **Drawing-style,** a drawing of a dog, like ones you see in a comic book.

So which representation would be the best? That is entirely up to you to find out. Before you reached the bullet points you may already have had an image of a dog in your head and that would be the image to use. Just go with the image that comes to mind. Sometimes it's a personal image, sometimes not. My image would be the German Shepherd, as that is the way I simply imagine dogs look like. I do have fond memories from my childhood as we did have a Pug and a Pekingese when I was growing up, but the appearance of these types of dogs are simply not how I imagine dogs. If I on the other hand had to memorize information specific about Pugs, then I would of course use the childhood memory of the Pug.

Independent of which type of images you use, you have to make sure of two things. One is that the image should be as detailed as possible. It is not enough to imagine a colorless stick-dog to make it memorable. You need to be able to visualize the dog! For example, I encountered a female employee in a local store a few weeks back. I could easily describe her as simply being attractive, but if I were to recall her looks again later, then I would not have much to go for from simply finding her attractive. Emma Watson is attractive and so is Taylor Swift. But it was neither of them standing in that store that day. If I on the other hand noted that she had blue eyes, long red hair, a mole on her left cheek and was wearing a blue silk scarf, then I am more likely to recall her in my memory. For that reason, I have the habit of memorizing four details of people I encounter in public.

So how can we describe the dog? Try visualizing the color of the fur or how its tongue hangs out of its mouth. Maybe its ears are pointing up because it is alert. You may even be able to imagine the dog, using your other senses. Can you hear it barking or smell its breath? Maybe you even imagine the soft feeling of your hand toughing the fur. Adding other sensory information, such as feeling heat or cold is also powerful senses to use. Images alone are quite memorable, but adding your other senses means that you have multiple ways to remember the dog. Also, as often as possible, try to make your mental images move. Moving images are usually remembered better than still-standing ones.

Exercise: Four Details Observation

The next time you meet someone else, note four details about this person so you are able to visualize him or her later. It could be the clothes they are wearing, the way their hair look, some special gestures in their face or an animal they remind you of.

The point of this exercise is to help your visualization skills. If you are in the habit of noticing details about someone or something, then you are able to imagine much more detailed mental images. It could of course also be useful to use this exercise with cars, buildings or animals to help you further. Additionally, it is a great social skill to be observant of others around you. Ever heard about the phrase "To be interesting you have to be interested"? Interest is actually an attractive trait for most women, which by the way is a great selling point if you have a lot of boys in the classroom.

Secondly, you must create some kind of context for the dog or involve it in a story. Why is it barking? Is it barking at you or is it trying to protect you from something else? Maybe it is a happy bark because it is happy to see you. Adding this kind of information to the images is helpful when you have to link the dog to other information later. This may be a little weird at first, but I can ensure you that it will be important later. One thing is for certain: kids are great at creating such memorable stories.

ABSOURDITY IS MEMORABLE

Somehow our brain has an easier time remembering absurd images than regular ones. Maybe it is because we are accustomed to the idea of something being funny or maybe we just have a hard time forgetting somethings out of the ordinary. Whatever the reason is, we can use this knowledge to our advantage. Our imagination is the powerhouse of our memory, so the more vividly we can imagine, the easier we will be able to create great images. A great way to do so is to give animals and inanimate objects human characteristics like arms and legs and the ability to talk. Just try and imagine how pissed your refrigerator is because you keep forgetting to close the door, so it smacks you with its fists.

It can also be helpful to imagine multiple uses for objects and here I have a little task for you. Go to your sock drawer and take out a sock, then set a timer for 3 minutes. In these 3 minutes, write down all the different ways this sock can be used.

...

How many uses did you find for the sock? The first time I tried this, I found 10 uses: glove, bandage, rag, cap, kindle, storage, use it to gag, strangle or hit someone, or use it to tie something together. These are all very straight forward usages and not very imaginative. Later I tried giving the same task to 10-year-olds and they enlightened me of how the sock could serve as a sleeping bag for mice or how a bird could roll it up and use it as a nest. The funniest response I got was probably that the Easter Bunny is quite small, so it had to put the eggs in a sock instead of a sack.

NUDITY IS MEMORABLE

When I was around 14 years old, I read a detective novel. I was in the habit of visualizing everything I read (though it was subconscious at that time), so I created a lot of mental images about this novel. The novel was not really that good, so most of the memories are gone now, but there is one image that still stick – even after more than 15 years has passed. A female reporter had been kidnapped and the protagonist had to save her. When he arrived, he found the woman tied up naked in the corner of the room, while the kidnapper sat in an armchair. The amazing thing about this memory is not that I remember a naked woman created from my imagination, but that I remember most of what happened in that scene. I remember how the detective came in through the door, fought with the kidnapper and released the reporter from the restraints. I also remember how he put his jacket around her and how she was seemingly too occupied writing an article about her experience than covering herself up.

Even though the content in this book is directed to the teaching of kids and young people, I will still share this with you: sexual images are very effective memory boosters! Maybe it is because sex is one of our basic instincts or maybe it is just because nudity is interesting for most people. Whatever the reason is, they are proven to be powerful.

If you are a timid person or just don't want to promote imaginary nudity in your classroom, then you of course don't have to. Some kids, mostly boys but also girls, realize by themselves how some objects and concepts associate well with body parts and nudity, as you will see when I show you some student responses in chapter 6. Should the students make such mental images, you shouldn't try to stop them from using them. Memorization and association are about using the images that comes most naturally to the students and if nudity is one of them, then let them use it to their advantage.

VIOLENCE IS MEMORABLE

Another powerful memory booster is violence. If you have ever experienced something violent happening in real life, then you should know. This could be a car accident you were involved in or witnessing. Such memories aren't easily forgotten, and we can use that to our advantage.

I do not, by any means, want to encourage you or your

students to use any traumatizing images to boost your memory – this could even end up having the opposite effect. What I instead want you to use is what I call "fun violence". Have you ever watched the rabbit season VS duck season scene with Bugs Bunny, Daffy Duck and Elmer Fudd? Elmer Fudd is going to shoot either Bugs or Daffy and they are both trying to convince him to shoot the other. Bugs tricks Elmer Fudd to shoot Daffy, causing Daffys' beak to spin around his head. That is what I mean by "fun violence". You can use such violent images to create small fun situations which can be quite memorable.

Using violence in memorization, doesn't necessarily mean that we need to create scenes from Tom & Jerry or Loonie Tunes. Violence could also be imagining someone (or something) falling down the stairs or a car crash. An example from one of my own memory systems is that I imagine Don Eppes (Numb3rs) trying to kick a football on the top of the stairs at my local gym. He misses, loses his balance and falls down the stairs, sounding like a drum hitting each step.

REMEMBERING CONCEPTS

Imagining a dog is not hard for most people, but what if I asked you to imagine an electrical current? Multiple? Full? Hanging? This is where it becomes tricky for most, because those concepts do not have physical form, so here context is important.

Electrical current gives me an image of an electrical cord. To remember that it is a current and not a cord, I enlarge the image, so it is as big as a tunnel and then I fill it with water. The water is running through the tunnel (the cord) creating a current. I also imagine lightning below the surface to demonstrate that the current is electric. In your own image, you could remove the water from my image and only have a current of lightning running through the tunnel, or not have a tunnel at all and just imagine a normal cord where you see a spark move from one end to another. Using Pikachu as the image for electricity is also something I have seen been used – again, it is all about using our imagination.

To demonstrate the concept of multiple, let's stay with the dog from before. First and foremost, what are there multiple of? If there are multiple dogs, then we can simply imagine multiple dogs surrounding us. If the dog is suffering from multiple sicknesses, then we can imagine it with a thermometer in its mouth and a bandage around its tail. Dogs don't use thermometers but remember that it is about creating memorable objects. The more absurd the better!

The concepts of full and hanging can be used the same way as with the dog. We can imagine a glass full of dogs or maybe the dog drank so much water that the water is flowing out of its ears. How is the dog hanging? Is it hanging on the edge of a cliff or is it (god forbid) getting hanged?

It is not a bad idea to have a stand-alone image for words such as multiple, full and hanging. Here I normally use general objects and add some movement to it. I have multiple Russian nesting dolls jumping out from one another, a glass overflowing with water and an apple hanging on a thin branch.

ASSOCIATION IN THE CLASSROOM

When applying the principles from this chapter in your lectures, you can choose to either teach the students about association directly, or simply include it in your own explanations. Just be aware that skipping the part where the students create their own mental images will also skip the storage stage in the three stages of memorization. Teaching the students how to make their own mental images based on their own associations, allows the students to actively take part in the storage stage, greatly enhancing their ability to store the information in their long-term memory.

Teaching the principles of creating mental images can be tricky without the right context, so I usually teach it in correlation with the Numbershape system. The lesson plan for a 90 minutes introduction to the use of memorization techniques can be found in chapter 7.

Exercise: What Color is a Subject?

This is a question that creates an informal discussion between the students. It gives them awareness of association, because it makes the students think about other ways of looking at the subject than the traditional way. Most students agree that biology is green, because they associate the subject with plants, but there can come some interesting responses from some students. For example: some students think history is gray like a colorless photography while others think it is brownish like the color of old paper.

Chapter 5

The Memory Palace

The period which for us is known as the Ancient Greece has always been well-known for art, storytelling and philosophy. It was during this time legends about gods and heroes were born and spread across all of Greece by poets and storytellers. One of them was a poet named Simonides of Ceos.

A popular story about Simonides states that he was attending a banquet in the palace of a wealthy nobleman named Scopas. Simonides was well known for his engaging poetry, so he was summoned to the banquet to entertain the diner guests with stories and poems which he had composed in the honor of the host.

Sometime during the banquet, he was called outside at the request of two young men. In his absence the banquet hall collapsed, crushing Scopas himself and all his dinner guests to death. The friends and families wanted to bury the bodies of their loved ones but that proved to be challenging as rocks and rubble had mangled many of their corpses beyond recognition.

Then it turns out that Simonides was able to identify each corpse by its location based on a memory he had of the dining guests sitting around the table. In the end, all the deceased would receive proper burials with the help of Simonides. The memory Simonides used to recall each corpses face and location is said to lay the foundation of the memory technique which today is known as the Memory Palace.

SPATIAL MEMORY

One of the principles of memorizations is to make use of our strengths instead of trying to force information to stay in our brain. The memory from the story about Simonides of Ceos seem to come easy to him, and when we think about it, it actually makes sense that he was able to memorize the physical location or each person. What he did was making use of something called spatial memory. We use the spatial memory when we navigate through a forest, a city or even a room. We also use it to remember where objects are located physically. Finding our way around a location and remembering where things are within it has been crucial for survival back in the days, and therefore our brains are still great at remembering locations.

Think for example about the route you take when you go to work. Do you have to use Google Maps to find your home every day? Think also about your working space. If you have bookshelf is it then on the left side or the right side of your desk? Such simple memories easily stick to our brain and the same can be said for the students. If you ask them about the route they took when they went to school this morning, then they have no problem giving you an answer – even if they are unable to remember the topic you taught them five minutes earlier. They may even be able to remember what happened at certain points along the way, from when they left their home to they entered the classroom. This is because a journey through a space gives structure to the otherwise cluttered collection of memories in our head. In other words: it helps us keep the memories in order like a filing cabinet. Using this knowledge of how spatial memories works, we can make use of this very practical memorization technique called the Memory Palace.

A Memory Palace is a spatial memory, normally created by imagining a physical location that you are familiar with. It doesn't have to be a palace, or even a building. It just has to be a location you know very well. Try and close your eyes and imagine the route you take from the school entrance to the teacher lounge. Can you do that? In that case, you already have what it takes to create a Memory Palace.

CHOOSING A LOCATION

The first step in creating a Memory Palace is to choose a location that is easy for you to recall in your mind. It could be the teachers' lounge, a classroom or your own house. It could also be a location outside or even a fictional location from a game or movie. Then you will plan a journey throughout this location which will be logical for you to take. It doesn't have to be the quickest route to go from point A to point B, it just has to be natural.

This means that:

- You will not be able to walk through walls or fly
- You will not be able to teleport to the other side of the location

Furthermore, for this technique to work you also have to make sure that:

- You don't cross the same path twice
- You will not end up in a dead end

Along this journey you will select a number of stations, one for each piece of information you are going to memorize. If you for example need to remember a simple shopping list consisting of seven items, then select seven spots along the journey which can suitable as stations. The order in which each station appears on the journey is crucial if you have to use the Memory Palace to memorize something in a specific order, like a sequence of numbers or something sorted by size.

BAD LOCATIONS CAN CAUSE BAD MEMORY

In the last chapter I mentioned briefly that bad or traumatizing memories can have the opposite effect when we are using a memory technique. The same is true for a location. When selecting a location for your Memory Palace, it is advisable to only use places of which you don't have any bad memories. Thinking about a location where something bad happened to you will sometimes remind you about the events and that can be a problem for different reasons. For one thing, it is not a good feeling to be reminded of something bad, but it can also disturb the memory you are trying to create.

I encountered this problem a few years back. I was sitting in my car waiting for a traffic light to turn green, when the driver in front of me suddenly decided to put his car in reverse, ramming directly into my car. I was not hurt by this episode, but it was a very negative experience. Aside from the shock of him hitting my car, I had to endure multiple threats and go through multiple authorities before getting him to rapport the damage to his insurance company so I could get my car fixed. The traffic light in which the event occurred was used in one of my Memory Palaces. Afterwards, I found that I had a hard time recalling the mental images placed in this traffic light, because the memory of the accident was much more memorable than the mental images I had used.

THE STORY OF THE FIVE OCEANS

To understand the full concept of this technique, I will here remonstrate how we can use a Memory Palace along with mental images to memorize the top five largest oceans in order of size. According to my information, they are:

- The Pacific Ocean
- The Atlantic Ocean
- The Indian Ocean
- The Southern Ocean
- The Arctic Ocean

The first step is to select a location that is easy for us to recall. It is always easier to understand this technique when both the teacher and the student are familiar with the location, so for the sake of this demonstration I will use Monica's apartment from Friends and hope that you at least are familiar with the general layout.

In this location we will determine a route which will be logical for us to take. Along this route we will select 5 stations (one for each ocean).

In this example I choose

1. The area around the kitchen

2. The area around couch

3. The area around the TV and Rachel's room

4. The platform area around Monica's room

5. The area around the bathroom

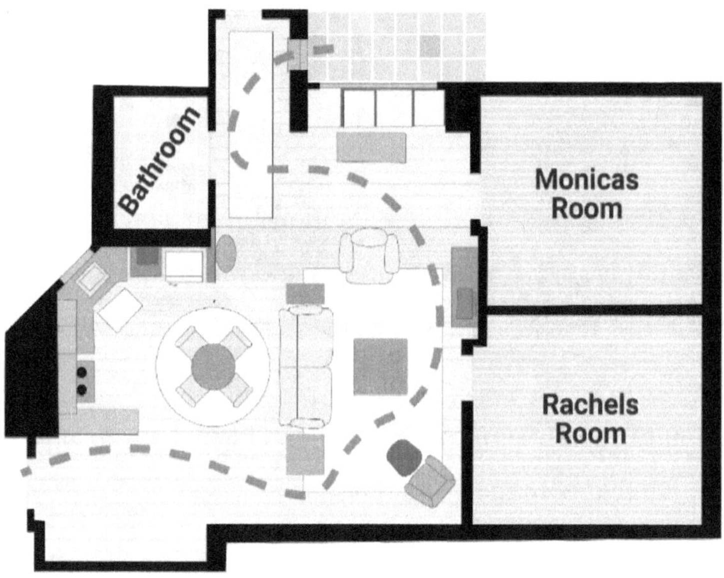

Now we have five stations, so we can begin storing our information. Let's start out with the biggest ocean: the Pacific Ocean. Which mental image can we use to remember this particular ocean? "Pacific" is a way to describe that something is peaceful, so I think of a hippie. I imagine this hippie making pancakes in Monica's kitchen. He is dressed in a long colorful shirt and wears a purple headband. His eyes are hidden behind his round-shaped Ozzy Osbourne-style sunglasses. I can hear the sound of the frying pan and as he throws the pancake up into the air, I can see a peace sign on the pancake. Besides the smell of pancakes, I can also smell grass and incense coming from the kitchen.

Next up, we have the Atlantic Ocean on the couch. The first image that comes to mind when I think of the word Atlantic is the movie poster of the movie Atlantis the lost empire. More specifically I think about the main character Milo James Thatch – so I imagine him sitting on the couch in his olive undershirt with both legs resting on the coffee table.

Then we have the Indian Ocean. Here we have a lot of options to choose from, as we probably have a lot of mental images associated with India. When I think of India I think of a bald, Buddhist monk, dressed in red ropes, so I place a Buddhist monk on top of the TV-set. He is meditating with his eyes closed and sitting cross-legged with his arms out to the side. I imagine sweet Indian music coming from the TV, creating an atmosphere of peace and tranquility.

We have come to the Southern Ocean. Here I imagine a stereotypical Texan ranch owner. He is big, wears a light-colored cowboy hat, light-blue shirt and lose jeans. On his feet he has big dusty brown boots, dragging dirt in front of Monica's bedroom. In the air I can catch the smell a cigarette he has just light. As I move past him, he starts speaking to me in a southern accent, telling me how nice and neat there is in Monica's apartment.

Finally, we have the Arctic Ocean. The Arctic is a cold region and who do we find in cold places? Eskimos! So, I imagine an Eskimo waiting to use the bathroom. He is wearing a big furry coat with the hood covering his ears. The floor around the bathroom is covered by a thin layer of snow to create a polar atmosphere. As I get near him he smiles and waves to me with his small red-gloved hands. He tells me that had to open the window because he thought it was too hot in here (why didn't he just take off the coat??), so I imagine feeling the cold as well.

So, this is how we use a Memory Palace. Try and think about my story and see if you can recall the five oceans in order from the largest to the smallest. This demonstrates just how powerful a Memory Palace can be. If we ever need the information, all we have to do is think back on Monica's apartment and how each of these weird people interacted with you and the surroundings. Now, if you are as familiar with Friends as I am, you may even imagine situations where Monica would interact with the five people. Making a mess in the kitchen, feet on the table, sitting on the TV and dragging dirt in on the floor – Monica would probably freak out and demonstrate some of the "fun violence" I talked about in the previous chapter.

USE YOUR IMAGINATION

It can be hard choosing a location to fit with the information we want to store. For example, what does Monica's apartment have to do with the five oceans? Nothing. But if we use our imagination a little, we can adjust the location to match the information we want to store. For example, could we imagine the apartment as we know it from the TV show and then imagine what it would look like if the whole place was flooded. I imagine that the floor is covered in a knee-deep layer of water, and it is "raining" from the ceiling. Maybe the tenant upstairs forgot to turn off the water or maybe the whole city of New York is flooded. It doesn't matter what the reason is, as long as we just imagine that it happened. This change in the location would of course also affect the way our five people interacted with their surroundings. The Texan ranch owner could be cursing because his clothes are soaked and the floor around the Eskimo would be covered by ice instead of snow. He could also be ice skating instead of just standing there waving. You are only limited by your own imagination!

A neat trick when using our imagination this way, is reusing the same location for multiple memory palaces. The appearance of the flooded version of Monica's apartment is different from the original version, so we can easily store other information in the version we are not using. We can also imagine other things that has happened to the apartment, like the floor covered with sand or the whole place being ablaze.

THE REVERSED MEMORY PALACE

Sometimes we may need the to recall the information in a reversed order, for example if we need to rank the oceans from the smallest to the largest. This would not be any harder than it would be for the students to find their way home from school. All they have to do is to reverse the journey they took coming to school this morning. The same applies for the journey throughout a Memory Palace. In the example with the five oceans, we would simply start the journey at the bathroom with the Eskimo and end the journey in the kitchen where the hippie is making pancakes. Reversing the journey can sometimes be a great way to evaluate whether we are using the Memory Palace to recall the information or if we have repeated the information so many times that it accidently has been memorized by rote learning.

MICRO MEMORY PALACE

Our spatial memory is not only limited to navigating around a location. It also tells us how physical objects are located in relation to each other and us. For example, while writing this chapter I have three things on or around my desk that are fixed at these specific locations. Even when I am away from the desk, I am able to recall all the objects and their locations: My monitor on the left side, my tablet station to the right side and right above it I have a small whiteboard. Because I know where each object is located, I can use my desk as the location of a Micro Memory Palace. The principle is the same as with the bigger one we used in Monica's apartment: only we shrink the mental images down so they can fit on smaller stations. The journey is typically just following the objects from the left side to the right and then using all parts of the objects that makes sense. For example, I can use the left side of the monitor by imagining something climbing up, the top of the monitor by imagining something moving across and the right side of the monitor by imagining something jumping or falling down.

The way I use Micro Memory Palaces is mainly to free up my short-term memory by storing small pieces of information that I need immediately like phone numbers, time or dates.

MEMORY PALACE IN THE CLASSROOM

When I teach students about the Memory Palace, I combine it with the Numbershape System which will be covered in the next chapter. I start out by choosing a location and the obvious choice while teaching in a school would of course be the school. Then I identify a route from the school entrance to another door leading outside. If it is a big school, I make sure that it is a route that is close to the classroom in which I am teaching so the students are familiar with the layout. I then take 10 pictures of 10 easily recognizable locations along the route so the students have 10 stations in which they can store information. These images are inserted in a Power Point, and as we talk about the route they are taking, I change the slides, so they know there to insert each piece of information. As I mentioned earlier, it helps if the teacher and the students use the same locations and it helps them understand the concept if they know exactly where to insert the mental images. If they get stuck in the process, I always encourage them to get out of the classroom and take a walk through the route.

Exercise: The Short-Term Memory Tester

Find a memory game – if possible one with detailed images. Remove all duplicates so you only have one of each card. The recommended number of cards is between 25 and 49

Show two cards to the students. After an agreed amount of time shuffle the cards together with the others and place them on a table with the picture side up. The task for the students is to identify the cards which they were shown before. As the game progresses, more and more cards will be shown to the students.

This exercise challenges the student's short-term memory, as they have to instantly recall the cards which they have just been shown. As the students becomes familiar with creating mental images and Memory Palace, this game can be used as a sort of evaluation to see how well they understand the concepts.

Chapter 6

The Numbershape System

In chapter 4 you learned how to use your imagination to link a mental image to information. As this is the foundation in the whole memory process, I am teaching you in this book, it can feel vivid and unappealing for the students. It is not enough to simply tell someone that mental images can improve their memory, especially because you probably will be met with a negative bias from the students, especially older students as well as their parents. So, we have to ask ourselves: what can we teach them to memorize that will make them realize how powerful memorization techniques are? The answer for me is numbers.

Numbers are not natural, as they only consist of a symbol without any special meaning to it. Telling a kid to imagine an apple, and they will have a mental image of an apple.

Telling a kid to imagine the number 2, and they will probably only think of the number 2. The number 2 has no smell, no feeling and it is probably colorless, so it is easier forgotten than the apple. The number 2 is not natural, it is a symbol made up by humans, so our brain is not accustomed to memorizing such information. So, what we need to do is to make a mental image to replace the number 2 in our memory. For this I use two memory systems:

- The Numbershape System
- The Dominic System

Both of these systems are useful to memorize numbers, but the memorization process to master each of them are quite different. The Dominic System is an advanced system that takes a lot of time to master, while the Numbershape System easily can be created, personalized and applied in a Memory Palace within 90 minutes. For this reason, I believe that it is convenient for both the students and you as the teacher to teach the Numbershape System together with the Memory Palace.

THE NUMBERSHAPE SYSTEM

The Numbershape System is easy to master, because all we have to do is to create 10 mental images, representing the numbers 0-9. The best system is the one you create yourself rather than one supplied for you and the same goes for the students. This is because the mind of each individual is varied so you and your student's associations between the numbers and the mental images are generally different from mine and everyone else's. The associations and images you generate from your own imagination will last far longer and be much more effective than any that is simply "stolen". Remember how I felt about pre-made mnemonics in the beginning of the book?

The construction of the system is not hard, because all you have to do is to look at the shape of the numbers 0-9 and then link mental images that reminds you of the numbers shape. For example, if we go back to the number 2, then I find that most people associate the shape of the number 2 with the shape of an elegant swan swimming in the water. By thinking about the number 2, they also think about a swan, and by thinking about a swan they also think about the number 2.

Whenever I teach the Numbershape System to students, I always show them what my images looks like. I emphasize for them that they will benefit more by creating their own systems than using mine, but that they are free to use some of my Number Shapes or maybe find some inspiration in them. I always tell them to use good visual images, with lots of good color and potential to use other senses.

MICHAEL'S NUMBERSHAPE SYSTEM

STUDENT EXAMPLES

0   Planet, Different kind of balls, Giant eye

1   Pen, Cane, Penis, Spear

2   Duck, Earpiece, Hanger

3   Mustache, Breasts, Butt

4   Chair, Flag, Folded napkin

5   Hook, Dragon, Hose

6   Bend golf club, Cherry

7   Pipe, Boomerang, Fishing Pole, Hook

8   Hourglass, Woman body, Glasses

9   Balloon on a string, Yoyo

VIOLENCE AND NUDITY

I have previously explained how violence and nudity can be used as strong memory boosters which we can use to our advantage. My choice of violent images in my own system (the batarang, bomb and axe) is because they create memorable situations when they interact with the location in my Memory Palace.

As you can see in the student examples, I have sometimes taught students who made associations about nudity. A funny situation I once had was a student who used a penis as the Numbershape for the number 1. I met him about 6 months later, where he told me that he had used it in a Memory Palace afterwards. This resulted in him being haunted by a giant penis growing out from the door every time he walked through the room he had used as a location. He told me that he was not sure if he was just very good at using memory techniques or if he was somewhat disturbed, but he definitely had no problem remembering where the number 1 belonged in that Memory Palace.

NUMBERSHAPES IN THE CLASSROOM

It usually doesn't take long for the students to create their personal Numbershape System or learn how to use a Memory Palace (especially if we follow the procedure described in the next chapter), so I usually ask the students to apply the techniques right away, by memorizing the number 3141592653. I don't tell them what the number is, but sometimes they figure out right away that they are about to memorize the first part of pi.

Using the first picture of the Memory Palace I start out by telling them a little story of how I came to the school this day and had to dodge a batarang (Batmans boomerang, my number 3) flying through the air which ended up getting stuck in the window. I include as many senses as I possibly can in this scene, including the sound of glass breaking. Afterwards I show them the next picture in the slide and explain how they have to create a scene on this location where they include their number shape for the number 1. By this point they should understand the technique and can solve the task on their own. Sometimes they limit their own imagination on what is realistic and then it is up to us teachers to show them that it is okay to make the flag pole break up from the floor or make the swan yell at them for running in the hallway.

OTHER SYMBOLS

The principles in creating Numbershapes are applicable when working with other symbols as well. Though it may be challenging for students, they can create mental images on each letter of the alphabet. It is not too relevant though, as letters usually are represented in a word, so it would be better to memorize the meaning of the word instead of memorizing the individual letters. If you are teaching students that are especially fond of math and physics, then they may have fun creating images for symbols, such as π, Δ and θ.

Chapter 7

Memory in the Classroom

The approach to teaching memorization techniques can feel a little alien compared to teaching the subject of math or history. Teachers are not given tools to create a lesson plan to improve the student's short-term memory or long-term memory. Usually teachers are simply provided with some small hacks or pre-made mnemonics they can show the students. Pre-made mnemonics can be useful in the encoding process of memorization, but if we want the students to improve their memory, we need to teach them how to create their own memory systems.

I myself have directly taught the students how to use Numbershapes and Memory Palace to memorize a sequence of 10 numbers. In this chapter I will therefore give you a quick glimpse of my own personal 90-minute lesson plan, which you can customize as you want. The goal of the lesson is not for the students to be able to memorize that specific number but instead to give them a fundamental understanding of how their memory works. The lesson can therefore include in any subject – not only in math.

I have mainly taught students aged between 13 and 16, so I have limited experience with younger students. They are just as capable to learn the techniques, though the whole approach you take to teaching them about the system is entirely up to you.

INTRODUCTION

The first thing I do is to test the students by showing them a number they need to memorize. The number I usually show them is

$$3141592653$$

Some students may immediately recognize this as the mathematical constant, pi. The number will be visible on a PowerPoint slide for around 10 seconds. Afterwards I ask the students how much they remember of the number. In this demonstration the students use encoding to try and memorize the number, so they will rely on vision, acoustic and semantic. You may notice some of the students silently moving their libs to try and encode the number in their memory while others look for patterns. Patterns in this specific number could be how the number starts and ends with the number three, how the number 5 is the fifth number in the sequence and how 14 is followed by 15. Those who recognize that the number is pi, may already know the first three numbers, as 3,14 is the constant they work with in geometry.

SIMONIDES OF CEOS

After the demonstration I tell the story of Simonides of Ceos. In chapter 5 I outlined the main points of the story, but feel free to recreate the story – just remember this is not a history lesson! At this point I don't emphasize the power of the spatial memory, as I want the student to create their Numbershapes before introducing them to the Memory Palace. Instead I tell the students how mental images can be much easier to remember than numbers, mostly because numbers are "boring".

THE NUMBERSHAPES

The principle of Numbershapes is easily understood by most students. The hardest part in most cases is to not limit their own imagination. To show how I create a Numbershape, I draw the number two on the whiteboard and add some characteristics of a swan, like the head and the wing.

Then I show the students the 10 images from page 61, so they can find inspiration in my approach. The number 4 can be tricky for some students, so I remind them that they can write it as an open number four or a closed number four.

The time it takes to create the images depends on the students, but in my experience, they only need 15-20 minutes. The process of which the students find the images are entirely up to them. Some students find pictures on the internet, some students make colorful illustrations and others brainstorm in groups. It is not wrong to work together in groups, as long as each student make their own personal associations.

THE MEMORY PALACE

After the students are done creating their Numbershapes, I ask them to return to the classroom. Here, I ask the students if they remember the story about Simonides of Ceos and ask some of them to explain what he used to identify the deceased people (here I am fishing for the location). I then randomly select students to demonstrate the effect of the spatial memory, by telling them to close their eyes and point in the direction of objects in the classroom, like the door and the whiteboard. Reminding the students how they use their spatial memory on their way to school each day is also great in this stage.

After this short demonstration, I explain the main principles of creating a Memory Palace (basically it is all about imagining a route throughout a location we are familiar with and place the mental images along the route). As mentioned earlier, it is much easier to teach Memory Palace if the teacher and student are both familiar with the location, so for this reason I have already prepared the location to be a route through the school. Along the route I have taken pictures of 10 places which would make sense to use as stations. These 10 pictures are shown in the PowerPoint, while I explain the route they take. Afterwards I demonstrate on the first picture how they can use the Numbershape of number three to link the number 3 to this station. The visual use of the pictures makes this concept easy to understand.

Next, I task the students to memorize the same number from the introduction, but this time they have to use their Numbershapes and the Memory Palace to memorize the number. Again, the process they use are different from students to students. Some students draw a map, some student walk along the route and others create the Memory Palace in their mind. This process forces the students in the storage stage, to store the number to the long-term memory.

EVALUATION

Finally, it is time to evaluate. This evaluation serves two purposes. First and foremost, it tells us teachers how well the students understand the memorization techniques, but it also demonstrates the power of using the techniques for the students. The test I give the students is to recall the whole number that they were asked to memorize, but with a little twist: I want them to recall the number in reversed order! This eliminates errors in case the students have been repeating the number so many times that they accidentally have been using rote learning and therefore still are in the encoding stage. The procedure they need to use is to simply imagine walking through the location in the reversed order, starting with the last station. If they are able to recall the whole number in reversed order, then it means that they probably understand how to create and use a Memory Palace.

FURTHER TEST AND DISCUSSIONS

Depending on how much time there is left, I sometimes ask the students how they imagine they can use the techniques they learned. Common responses are phone numbers and pin codes, but with a little help they may realize they it can be used to memorize objects besides numbers, like grocery lists. I then ask them how they would memorize a list consisting of three common things like milk, eggs and carrots.

Chapter 8

The Dominic System

Of the many memory champions who have emerged throughout history, few can say that they have been able to match the British Dominic O'Brien. After watching a program on TV where someone memorized a whole deck of cards, he found an interest in memory techniques. As a student he was diagnosed with dyslexia and had a general problem reading and writing, but that did not hold him back from winning his first World Memory Championship in 1991. But he did not stop there. In total he has won the World Championship eight times and come in second twice. At the supposed end of his career he managed to get a sixth place as well, before he decided to retire from the competition. In the recent years he has returned to game, by winning the World Senior Memory Championships three years in a row, from 2017 to 2019. At the time of you reading this book he may even have more titles on his belt.

No one in the history of Memory World Championships has ever held so many titles as Dominic O'Brien – the kid who was diagnosed with dyslexia. Besides the titles, he is also known as a major innovator in the field of memory techniques, as he was the one who created the number memorization system known as the Dominic System.

CONVERTING NUMBERS TO LETTERS

The Dominic System is a mnemonic system used to memorize sequences of numbers. The system works the same way as the Numbershape System, where we convert numbers to mental images which you place in a Memory Palace, but the memorization procedure and conversion steps used in the Dominic System are far more complex.

The first step in creating your own Dominic System is to convert the numbers 00-99 into pair of letters (numbers below 10 includes a zero: 01, 02...).

The conversion method used is entirely up to you, but the conversion commonly used goes like this:

Number	0	1	2	3	4	5	6	7	8	9
Letter	O	A	B	C	D	E	S	G	H	N

The letters A, B, C, D, E, G and H follows the numerical order in which the letters appear in the alphabet. I find that most students can easily convert the first five letters, while G and H can be a little challenging. Here you can show the students how the shape of number 7 appears in the shape of the letter G and how the letter H looks like an incomplete digital number 8. S and N are used because of the sound they make when you say the numbers 6 and 9 out loud, but the letters F and I could be just as valid substitutes as long as it works. The number 0 is represented by the letter O, because of its shape.

FINDING THE IMAGES

When connecting the numbers to mental images, you have to first break the numbers 00-99 into 100 pairs of two digits. This way you will end up with 100 pairs of letters which has to be converted to mental images, making this system a little more time consuming than the Numbershape System.

Each pair of digits represents an individual doing a certain action. For example, for the number 86 (HS) in my Dominic System I use Homer Simpson as my mental image and his action is that he is eating a giant donut. This action is unique in my system, so I get reminded by Homer Simpson and the number 86 from this action alone.

There are different ways to make the associations. If you can make a direct association between the number and a person, then that would be great. An example could be 07 reminding you of James Bond or 00 reminding you of a melding snowman. I am not interested in sports myself, but I believe making direct associations with your favorite athletes' number could also work.

The numbers that doesn't have an immediate association with an image can be assigned images by using the pair of letters as the initials of people, like Homer Simpson from before. Some numbers also represent part of names, like HE which reminds me of Hercules (Disney's Hercules) and NE which reminds me of Negan (The Walking Dead).

In my own Dominic System, I have two unique associations. One is 49 which reminds me of an online platform called Dueling Network which again converts to a person I know who spent a lot of time on that platform.

49 ⟶ DN ⟶ Dueling Network ⟶ Gamer

Another example is 09 which represents Gyro Gearloose's assistant, Little Helper (Disney's Donald Duck universe), based on how his head is "turned on". If you try to find logic in my Dominic System, he will be the most far-fetched character, but for me he is perhaps the most memorable.

09 ⟶ ON ⟶ Little Helper ⟶

Some of my associations, like 12, also needs a few extra steps before they make sense to others. Previously when I tried to make an association with AB I thought of Alibaba from the fairy tales, but for some reason I had a hard time visualizing him. After I began trading in the stock market, the poor visualization of Alibaba was replaced by an image of Jack Ma, who is the man behind the company Alibaba Group. Jack Ma is easy for me to visualize, so I replaced the

Alibaba from the fairy tales with Jack Ma.

12 ⟶ AB ⟶ Alibaba ⟶ Jack Ma

GUIDELINES FOR CHOOSING IMAGES

Dominic O'Brien recommend using people (or at least something that has a human shape) when creating the system. The reason for this is that we sometimes encounter situations where one person from your system has to person the action of another person (this will be explained more in depth when I show you how to memorize four-digit numbers). In other words, all actions must be performable by all the other characters in our Dominic System. My Dominic System is filled with martial artists, like my number 57 Eddie Gordo (Tekken) who is performing a Brazilian Capoeira Dance, so I need all the other people in my system to be able to perform this dance as well. This would exclude anything that doesn't have the human shape, like a lion, a car or a trash can. Homer Simpsons on the other hand would be able to perform the dance because he is human.

It is also important that the images and actions we use in our Dominic System are easy to distinguish from one another. For example, if you are a big fan of soccer, you may feel tempted to use multiple soccer players from your favorite team. The problem here is that all of them would probably use soccer as their action, so they would not have unique actions. That said, I have several associations of martial artists all performing different styles of martial arts. Number 62 is my Nunchaku-Do sensei, which fighting style I can distinguish from the Brazilian Capoeira performed by Eddie Gordo. This is of course based on my interest and past experience in martial arts.

Just like I do when teaching the Numbershape System, I always share my Dominic System with the students. I tell them to keep in mind that it is better to create their own associations. Copying mine or someone else's list would be difficult for them to remember, aside from famous characters and associated actions that they are already familiar with. Some of the people I use are people I know personally, so these would not make sense for others to use.

MICHAELS DOMINIC SYSTEM

		Person	Action	Known from
00	OO	Olauf the Snowman	Melting	Frozen (Disney)
01	OA	Ole Andersen	Jiu-Jitsu throw	My Jiu-Jitsu coach
02	OB	Orlando Bloom (Legolas)	Shooting arrows	Lord of the Rings
03	OC	LOC	Giving the finger	Danish musican
04	OD	Junkie	Overdosing	Steriotypical Image
05	OE	Ole Røn	Repairing computer	My former teacher
06	OS	Yoh Asakura	Creating an Oversoul	Shaman King
07	OG	OG LOC	Rapping	GTA San Andreas
08	OH	Raiden (Oh my god!)	Flying with lightning speed	Mortal Kombat
09	ON	Little Helper	Glowing lightbulb	Disney
10	AO	Aokiji	Freezing the ground	One Piece

11	AA	Anders And (Danish name for Donald Duck)	Angry yelling	Disney
12	AB	Jack Ma (Alibaba)	Meditating	CEO of Alibaba Group
13	AC	AC Slater	Exercising with dumbells	Saved by the Bell
14	AD	Albus Dumbledoor	Casting spell	Harry Potter
15	AE	Albert Einstein	Chalking a blackboard	Physicist
16	AS	Arya Stark	Water dancing	Game of Thrones
17	AG	Anne Groth	Playing guitar	Former teacher
18	AH	Anthony Hopkins (Hanibal)	Wearing mask	Silence of the Lambs
19	AN	Anette Nelleman	Sminking a person	Former teacher
20	BO	Bob Richards	Rolling around	Tekken
21	BA	Barch von Ronsenburg	Beam of black energy attack	Final Fantasy XII
22	BB	Bente Bentsen	Teaching German	Former teacher
23	BC	Bill Clinton	Waving	Former president

24	BD	Baek Doo San	Taekwondo kicks	Tekken
25	BE	Jakob Bentzen	Playing cards	Acquaintance
26	BS	Bud Spencer	Hitting people with chair	Actor
27	BG	Bill Gates	Throwing money	CEO of Microsoft
28	BH	Benny Hansen (Fede)	Eating with his hands	Danish actor
29	BN	Brian Nielsen	Boxing	Danish boxer
30	CO	Conan Edogawa	Super kick on soccer ball	Detective Conan
31	CA	Chris Anderson	Giving a TED talk	Author
32	CB	Capone Bege	Shooting bullets from his body	One Piece
33	CC	CC Babcock	Laughing like a maniac	The Nanny
34	CD	Charles Darwin	Boarding HTS Beetle	Biologist
35	CE	Charlie Eppes	Explaining math	Numb3rs
36	CS	Cloud Strife	Omnislash	Final Fantasy VII
37	CG	Carl Grimes	Killing zombie with hatchet	The Walking Dead

38	CH	Caroline Hansen	Happy Dancing	Acquaintance
39	CN	Carl Nielsen	Playing violin	Danish violinist
40	DO	Tony Do	Game-show laugh	Acquaintance
41	DA	David Addenborough	Scaring sloth	Natural historian
42	DB	Son Goku	Kamehameha	Dragonball
43	DC	Doctor Cid	Shooting with gunblades	Final Fantasy XII
44	DD	D.D. Warrior Lady	Vanish into dark dimension	Yu-Gi-Oh
45	DE	Don Eppes	Shooting with gun	Numb3rs
46	DS	Dorthe Svenstrup	Using chemestry	Former colleague
47	DG	Daniel Gilbert	Crawling down from a tree	Author
48	DH	Dennis Haskin (Mr. Belding)	"What is going on here?"	Saved by the Bell
49	DN	Yu-Gi-Oh player	Playing cardgame	Yu-Gi-Oh
50	EO	Egon Olsen	Robbing a bank	Olsenbanden
51	EA	EA sport	Playing soccer game	Steriotypical Image
52	EB	Elaine Bennes	Pushing people	Seinfeld

53	EC	Emilia Clarke (Daenerys Targaryen)	Riding a Dragon	Game of Thrones
54	ED	Elizabeth Do	Throwing cards	Acquaintance
55	EE	Queen Elizabeth Of England	Driwing rower	Queen of England
56	ES	Ed Sherren	Singing	Singer
57	EG	Eddie Gordo	Brazilian capoeira dance	Tekken
58	EH	Emil Hammerich	Hating the paperwork	Acquaintance
59	EN	Enel	Thunder Kirin	One Piece
60	SO	Samuel Oak	Giving pokedex	Pokemon
61	SA	Mr. Satan	Throwing exploding game boy	Dragonball
62	SB	Søren Brier	Using Nunchuks	My Nunchaku-Do coach
63	SC	Simon Craft	Seing the future	Numb3rs
64	SD	Scooby Doo	Wheel leg running scared	Scooby Doo
65	SE	Jerry Seinfeld	Comedy act	Seinfeld
66	SS	Adolf Hitler	Heiling	Schutzstaffel

67	SG	Athlete	Running	SG gym
68	SH	Shae	Nagging Tyrion	Game of Thrones
69	SN	Steen Nielsen	Evil smile	My former teacher
70	GO	Gary Oak	Throwing Pokeball	Pokemon
71	GA	Gagaga Cowboy	Shooting flames from revolver	Yu-Gi-Oh
72	GB	George Bush	Dodging shoes	Former president
73	GC	Gregor Clegane	Smashing rock/head	Game of Thrones
74	GD	Gold titan	Throwing gold	Heroes of Might and Magic III
75	GE	Genie	Coming out of a lamb	Alladin
76	GS	Gabriel Strokes	Praying	The Walking Dead
77	GG	Galileo Galilei	Looking through telescope	Physicist
78	GH	Ghandi	Meditating on mauntain	Ethicist
79	GN	Green Lantern	Using ring	Justice League

80	HO	Santa Claus (Ho ho ho)	Riding cane	-
81	HA	Hades	Light on fire	Hercules (Disney)
82	HB	Hanne Birgitte	Cooking	Former teacher
83	HC	HC Andersen	Writing a poem	Danish poet
84	HD	Holger Danske	Sitting on marmor brick	Danish statue
85	HE	Hercules	Lifting giant rock	Hercules (Disney)
86	HS	Homer Simpson	Eating Dounut	The Simpsons
87	HG	Hans Gundetofte	Slapping people	Acquaintance
88	HH	Hulk Hogan	Wrestling	Wrestler
89	HN	Niels Olsen (Horatio Nielson)	Acting with admiral costume	Ørkenens Sønner
90	NO	No Face	Trying to give gold	Spirited Away
91	NA	Nagamasa Azai	Scene from "Battle at Anagawa"	Samurai Warriors
92	NB	Noob Saibot	Using shadow teleportation	Mortal Kombat
93	NC	Nikolaj Coster-	Getting hand	Game of

		Waldau (Jamie Lannister)	chopped off	Thrones
94	ND	Napoleon Dynamite	Blowing up stuff with a dynamite	Napoleon Dynamite
95	NE	Nero the Sable	Teleporting on floating rocks	Dirge of Cerberus
96	NS	Newt Scamander	Keeping suitcase from opening	Fantastic Beasts and where to find them
97	NG	Negan	Hitting with baseball bat	The Walking Dead
98	NH	Napoleon Hill	Black and white broadcasting	Author
99	NN	Nina Williams	Shooting Bazooka	Tekken

The purpose of using associations is that they are easier to remember, but it does happen that some associations falls out of our minds. A way to make the associations more memorable would be to create a Memory Palace with 100 stations in which we insert each person performing their action. In case I forget the person I used for the number 83, then I think about the part of the park in which the 80s people are located and then I should be able to find HC

Andersen.

MEMORIZING TWO DIGITS

Memorizing two-digit numbers, like your seat in the train or your friend's house number, you just have to think of the person from your Dominic System performing his or her action in context with what you have to remember. For example, if I should remember that my seat number in the train is 97, then I imagine a giant Negan (The Walking Dead) knocking the train of the rails with a giant baseball bat. Notice that I don't just imagine him sitting in my seat. I chose to scale him up in size to make him more memorable. If I should use him to memorize my friend's house number, I would let him ravage my friends home.

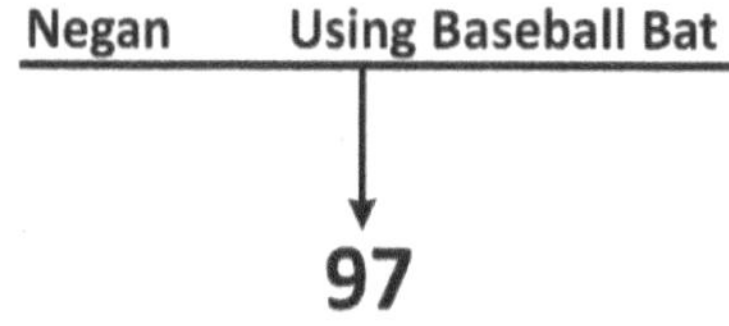

MEMORIZING THREE DIGITS

Memorizing three digits is not much more difficult than memorizing two digits. All you have to do is to use the first two digits from your Dominic System and then add the third number from your Numbershape System. If the house number I have to memorize is 975 I use Negan again, but instead of using his baseball bat, I imagine him using a giant snake instead.

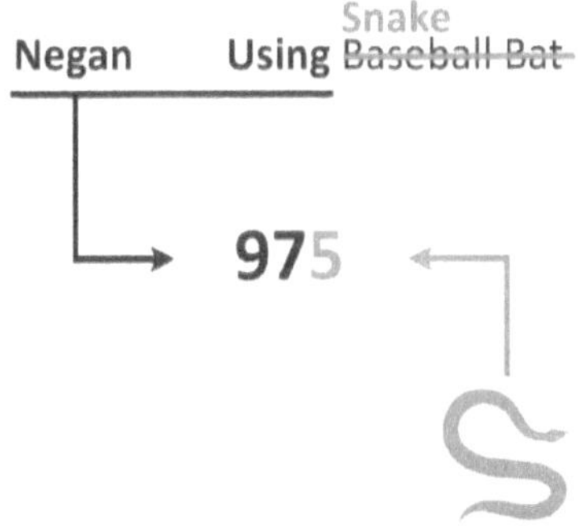

MEMORIZING FOUR DIGITS

Memorizing four digits is where the actions of the people in our Dominic System becomes important. The procedure starts out with splitting the four digits in pairs of two and then use the image of the character you have assigned to the first digit with the associated action for the second digit. You have previously read that I use a specific mental image to remember the number 7017. Here comes the explanation you have been waiting for!

The image I use is Gary Oak playing guitar. Why? Because Gary Oak is the person I association with the number 70 and "-playing guitar" is the action I associate with the number 17.

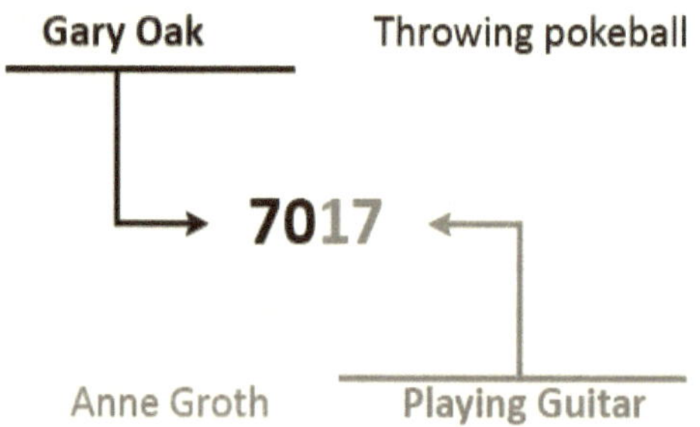

If I should not memorize 7017, but instead 7061, then the image I use would be Gary Oak throwing an exploding gameboy. All I did was to use the action "-throwing an exploding Gameboy" which is the action my number 61, Mr. Satan, performs. This is why it is important to be able to identify the person from the action alone. For this reason, each action should be performable by all the other characters.

MEMORIZING LONGER NUMBERS

When memorizing longer sequences of numbers, then the easiest way is to group the number together in clutches of four digits and then insert each image and association at stations in a Memory Palace. For example, if I should remember the number 141592653589, I would create three stations in a Memory Palace, containing the numbers 1415, 9265 and 3589. Using my Dominic System, I would imagine Albus Dumbledore writing the formula $E=mc^2$ on station one, Noob telling stupid jokes on station two and Charles Eppes acting with admiral costume on station three. Using these stations in the Memory Palace I am able to know in which order each group appear in the sequence.

THE DOMINIC SYSTEM IN THE CLASSROOM

The complexity and time consumption in creating a personal Dominic System raises the question of whether it should be taught in the classroom or not. To give the students an understanding of how mental images can be much more memorable than numbers, using the Numbershape System should be sufficient. There are of course those who wishes to learn more and improve their memorization skills, and for that purpose it is relevant that you as the teacher at least are familiar with the Dominic System, so you can provide the right guidance.

Chapter 9

Language Learning

In most languages a student's ability is determined by how well he or she can use the vocabulary and grammar. To master a language, we will need to memorize a whole dictionary of alien words and link them to the equivalent word in our own native language. Growing up in Denmark, I was taught how to speak German in school. Luckily some of the German words sound a bit similar in Danish, but some of the words we needed to imprint in out brain, following the standard "listen, repeat and use" procedure. As far as I know, this procedure has not improved much today. The job description of teachers has not yet extended to the "learning how to learn-procedure" that I feel is lacking in most subjects – language learning is no exception. No one really teaches the students how to store a large number of alien words and grammatical concepts in their long-term memory. Take the German word *das Mädchen* (girl). How are we supposed to remember that this noun is neutral and not feminine?

VOCABULARY

Since vocabulary is the basic building block of language, it is desirable and necessary to develop methods to learn and memorize words more easily. If you are teaching languages like Spanish, German or French, then you should know this to be true. Whenever possible, the students should be used to use their imagination to create a mental image of each new word they encounter. A lot of polyglots (speakers of multiple languages) I have talked to, has the habit of memorizing a fixed number of new words every day and use them in context after they have learned them. As with other memorization techniques the key word is association. Tony Buzan, the man behind Mind Mapping, has shared how he divide foreign words into three color categories:

Green for go ahead: these words are similar to the equivalent word in our native language. For example, the word *information* is the same in most European countries, so it is easy to remember.

Amber for wait and think: these words remind us of similar words in our native language, even though the words are not exactly the same. An example could be the Italian word *verde* (the color green). *Verde* is not the same in English, but we can easily make an association if we think about the English word *verdant*.

Red for stop, think and make a link: these words may have nothing in common with the equivalent word in our native language, which often comes as a big frustration for students. Here we need to play around with the word or the sound of the word and find a word or a phrase it resembles. For example, the Spanish word for *money* is *dinero*. *Dinero* sparks two associations in my mind; dinner and the actor Robert De Niro. Here you could use phrases like "you need money to buy dinner" or maybe "Robert De Niro has a lot of money" to create a link between *dinero* and *money*.

These three categories are described and used in the Collins Language Revolution Program (see bibliography at the end of the book).

Dividing the words like this, we can ease the learning process for students – especially struggling students. The words that are "amber" are interesting because they can lead the students to discover words in their own language that they were not even aware of. I experienced this myself as a kid when I encountered the other Scandinavian languages. Tons of words in Swedish and Norwegian would fall into the "green" and "amber" categories for a Danish student, because they are very similar to the Danish translations. In the end I ended up expanding my verbal library in the Danish language simply by learning the meaning of foreign words.

GENDERED NOUNS

One of the biggest pitfalls in language learning is grammar. I can speak from first-hand experience how frustrating it can be to learn the grammar of a language, especially if the grammar does not have fixed rules. In the German language, they have gender nouns which basically is three different ways to say "the" (der, die and das). Each word tells us whether the noun is masculine, feminine or neutral. This always bothered me as a student, because even though there were some guidelines to identify the gender it felt like there were a zillion exceptions to the rules. In the end it was all about memorization.

In my adult life I found that there is a simple way to remember the gender of nouns. All you need to do is to think of an image that reminds you of the noun and then use other associations to link the image with the respective gender. This association could be a color that reminds you of each gender. For example, if you need to remember that the German word *Löffel* (spoon) is masculine, then you can imagine a spoon with a strong masculine color, like blue. You would of course be well advised to use your imagination to make the spoon memorable, like giving it a face, arms and legs. You can further enhance this image, by giving the face a mustache. The word *Gabel* (fork) is feminine, so here you can imagine the fork with a feminine color, like red or pink. Additionally, you can think of the fork's teeth as a woman's eyelashes, like we did with spoons mustache. Finally, we have the word *Messer* (knife) which is neutral, so we would have to find a color which is somewhat neutral. I steer clear of colors like gray, black and white when I make associations, unless I want to be reminded that the knife is "boring", and boring stuff is rarely memorable. Instead I personally use green as a neutral (or natural) color. So, I imagine a light green knife with arms and legs. Enhancing a neutral noun is not always easy, but I find that giving the image a pacifier and if possible, a diaper works for me. Why? Because babies are neutral from birth as they have not yet been shaped to have an opinion. This approach of using colors to remember the genders can be used in other languages with gender nouns, so it is not exclusive to the German language.

By reading this part you have probably created some mental images in your mind, so can you remember the gender of the fork, spoon and knife?

HOW TO MEMORIZE A LANGUAGE

As I mentioned in the beginning of this book, I am not a language teacher, nor am I a polyglot at this point. I just have a great insight in a lot of European languages and an interest in learning. Still people come to me asking me how they can memorize a whole language and my answer is always the same: mental images and a Memory Palace.

I have already shown you how to use mental images to link a foreign word to a word that is somewhat similar in your native tongue. Let's get back to the German flatware set from before; *Gabel, Messer* and *Löffel.*

First of all, do you remember the gender of each word? Probably not. You may however remember the genders of the translations: fork, knife and spoon. All of these words fall into Tony Busan's "red" category, as we don't recognize any of them in the English language. So, we have to make strong associations to store them in our long-term memory.

I will start out with *Gabel* (fork). When I say the word out loud, I get reminded of the name Gabriel. Luckily for me, I know someone named Gabriel, so he is the one that comes to mind. Other likely candidates for me could be Gabriel Strokes (The Walking Dead) or the Archangel Gabriel. When you have your mental image or *Gabel*, you need to associate it with a fork or else there would be no point in remembering it. What I do is I imagine my acquaintance Gabriel holding a giant fork, which he swings around like a trident. Now, which gender was Gabel? It was feminine, so we need to make this image feminine by either changing the color or somehow make the fork or Gabriel more feminine. I imagine that the fork he is holding is a giant, pink, smooth plastic fork – not unlike one you would give a small child. On the fork I imagine a female face, where the eyes have long eyelashes and mascara and the libs are covered in dark red lipstick. This image is for me very memorable, but you have to make your own association to make it work for you.

Next, we have *Messer* (knife). Saying the word out loud I think of someone making "more of a mess". Other words could be message, messenger or messiah, but I stick with "more of a mess" because of my mental image. There is a special person I think of who is making "more of a mess" with a knife, and that is Jason Vorhees (Friday the 13th). This machete-wielding monster fits well with my Gabel-character from before, as they both are human-like, so they can interact with each other's in my Memory Palace. I imagine Jason "making a mess" of someone, while Gabel is approaching from behind, ready to attack. I have colored Jason light-green, like he has just taken a dive in an algae-filled lake. The purpose of this is of course to remind me that *Messer* is a neutral noun.

Finally we have *Löffel* (spoon) which proved to be quite challenging for me. I do have a childhood friend who named his dog Öffel, but I don't remember what the dog looked like, so I can't use it as a mental image. Let's instead look at the word itself. Saying the word out loud (it is pronounced loeffel) doesn't ring a bell either. So, we need to see if we can find something if we divide the word up in *loef-* and *-fel*. Here we may have something. *-fel* is somewhat similar to *fell*, so we can imagine something that has just fallen. Looking at the word *loef-*, I immediately imagine a loaf of bread. So, in my imagination, I have a loaf of bread which just fell down. Now, time to associate this with a spoon. I imagine a giant bread on the kitchen table shaped like a spoon. Along comes Jason and Gabriel from before and knocks down the bread, so it falls down and lands on the floor. The impact breaks the bread in two, revealing that the inside is not white, but instead light blue – like someone used food coloring to decorate the bread.

So, this was three associations between German and English nouns – also containing the gender. So, how do we make sure we can recall these images later? Obviously, we use a Memory Palace! I already hinted that I would place this brawl in the kitchen, because this is where I imagine that we find the flatware. The location for images I use to memorize German words is my mom's old house, because it was rather big.

Finally, a question that might emerge: if I am from Denmark, how come I don't use Danish associations? Good question! The answer is that I actually use both Danish and English translations, because it gives me a bigger repertoire of words I can use in my associations. The German word *bleibe* (to stay) is very similar to the Danish translation *blive*, so I have an easy time remembering that word while an English-speaking person would have to make an association.

Chapter 10

Fiction and Articles

Using memorization techniques, we can memorize most information, and that will of course include fiction as well as well as non-fiction literature. A commonality in both is that the students has to be able to identify the essence of the text and only create mental images that contains information about the overall plot or content. Using Memory Palaces to store the information is of course a great way to make sure the information if easy to recall at a later point.

FICTION

Fiction is perhaps the easiest form of text to memorize if we pay attention to what is happening. I have previously mentioned in this book how I imagined the story play out like scenes in a movie. Using some of the principles from chapter 4 we can easily create memorable images to help us recall the plot of a story. Depending on the level of which we have to be able to recall the plot, we can actively memorize the information by identifying the most important parts of the story and then play them as small scenes in a Memory Palace.

When memorizing the plot of a novel, it helps if we understand the shapes novels tend to take. In the beginning we usually have a teaser or introduction which gives us a glimpse into the story's universe. Then we have the elaboration, where we get to know the characters and the conflict which must be solved. From there, we have the whole process of solving the conflict, which usually ends in a battle or confrontation with the antagonist. There may be a moment of self-revelation during the conflict that helps the character defeat the antagonist. Obviously, not all stories use this exact structure, but categorizing the mental images like this can certainly help us memorizing the story.

In fiction we don't necessarily have to remember the names of the characters, because the author will use them over and over. In the end, we may come to identify with the characters and remember their names without effort. Some names are perhaps a little harder to memorize if they are out of the ordinary. An example is the potion master professor Slughorn from the Harry Potter universe. Who would keep a family name like that? In the Danish version, which I read as a child, he was named Schnobbevom (roughly translates to snobbish belly). These are weird names, but if we take the names apart, we can easily find mental images that fits in with the name. While reading the book, I always enlarged his stomach and made him look up in a snobbish manner to fit his name. For the original version of his name, it would be quite obvious to imagine him with two horns in the shape of slugs sticking out of his forehead like antennas. It gives some weird images, but it gets the job done.

ARTICLES

When students are working with articles, they are often expected to memorize facts and concepts. Here it is crucial that they have some background information about the topic discussed in the article so they can understand what it is about. Without the understanding there would be no point in memorizing the information.

The approach to memorizing articles is different than memorizing fiction. First and foremost, it is important that the students understand that it is not the number of words they convert to mental images that is important. Instead they should focus on creating mental images based on specific keywords or key phrases that contain the meaning of the article. In general, only 20% of the words in an article contains the knowledge needed to understand the information. The remaining 80% is non-keywords like *is, of, has, for, the* and *to*. These non-keywords contain no useful information but is instead used to link the text together, so it makes sense to the reader.

The keywords and key phrases are the ones we use when we find the point in the text. For each point we find, we can create a mental image which we can input in a Memory Palace. Let's for the sake of this demonstration use this short text which is part of an article I once wrote for biology students:

Lybia is a genus of small crabs that belongs in the family of mud crabs. They are better known as boxer crabs and pom-pom crabs. They are typically recognized for their remarkable cooperation with sea anemones. The crab attaches parts of a living sea anemone to its claws so that it can benefits from the paralyzing effect that the sea anemone has on other creatures, arming itself with a weapon for catching prey and defending against predators. The sea anemone benefits by being transported around the ocean floor, allowing it to capture food particles with its tentacles. This cooperation is not necessary for the survival of either the sea anemone or the crab as both can survive independent of each other's. It has also been observed that the boxing crabs can substitute the sea anemone with other organisms with similar effect, such as sponges or corals.

The first point in the article is that the boxer crab is small, belongs in the family of mud craps and has a name that somewhat gives it the appearance of a boxer or pom-pom girl. The image we can use is a crab with either pom-poms or boxing gloves. From top to bottom, we can imagine how the crab is covered in mud, similar to how criminals in an old western movie was covered in tar. Including the fact that it is small, should not mean that we need a small image. Instead imagine the crab shrinking on the spot in the Memory Palace.

The second point in the article is that they cooperate with the sea anemone, using it to catch prey and fend off predators. Here we can imagine the crap where the anemone is electric and expands from the crab's claws. If we should imagine it catching prey, we can imagine a small fish wrapped and electrocuted by the tentacle. To think of it fending off predators, imagine the tentacles hit a bigger, more dangerous-looking fish in the face like a whip.

The third point is the benefits the anemone gets by being transported around. Here I imagine the crab with a classic chauffeur cap, moving around a lot of tables. On each table is a plate with food which the anemone eat as the crabs moves around between the tables.

The last point is that the crab can use other organisms than the anemone, like sponges and corals. Here I imagine the crab walking around, but instead of the anemones, it is holding a normal washing sponge in one claw and a piece of coral in the other.

From this article I demonstrated four mental images. The number of images you should use is solely depending on how well you know the topic. You can probably deduce that the crab does not carry around the anemone for fun, but that it does it for a reason. If you know how sea anemones have a paralyzing effect on other animals, then you can probably also deduce that it is used for either attack, defense or both. Some students may have to create mental images to memorize or understand such facts while others can get by with few mental images.

MEMORIZING LONG TEXTS

It should not be expected of students to memorize the content of a whole book, but there are always those who want to take it a step further. In this case it is important that they are somewhat knowledgeable about their memory's rhythm, which will be elaborated in chapter 11. Basically, what they need to do is to stop at the end of each chapter or section and take some time reflecting over the information they have just read about. This is the perfect time to create the first draft of the mental images which can be used to memorize the information and will be reviewed later by the student.

Rhythm and Repetition

Learning effectively is not only about obtaining new information, it is also about being able to recall this information later. We can enhance our recollection by using the memory techniques described in this book, but it is still important to review and recall the information to be able to make it stick. I divide this into two parts: recall during learning and recall after learning. It is not necessary for the students to understand the principles in this chapter, but I have sometimes encountered students asking about this method, after which I have explained the concept. I will start out by making a quick comparison between those who use repetitions and those who do not.

Those who do not use repetitions are in danger of constantly learning new information but letting it slip out of their minds almost as fast as it got in. Such people will constantly have a hard time taking in new information which would require some background knowledge since this knowledge has been forgotten. Learning is not much unlike building a house: if the foundation slips, the whole structure of the house will collapse.

People who do review will find that whenever they encounter some new information that fits connects well with something they already have stored in their memory, then the new information will be learned more easily. This will create a positive cycle in which learning, understanding and recalling will assist each other, making the learning process smoother. The more we learn, the easier it is to learn more. If we return to the house building from before, then it would be equivalent to making sure that the foundation and walls are strong enough to support the construction of additional levels.

RECALL DURING A LEARNING PERIOD

In order to demonstrate how the memory works during a learning period, I will give you this little test. Before reading any further, please prepare a pen and paper for the next task.

At the bottom of this page you will find a list of words from the English dictionary. Read each word, one at a time without using any memorization techniques or reading the same word twice. The purpose of this test is to see how many words you can remember using your short-term memory alone. The order of which they appear is not important in this test. After you have completed reading the list of words, write down as many of the words as possible from your memory.

past	toward	minus
mostly	the	low
round	from	divide
behind	possible	against
considering	the	since
within	Disney	violent
multiply	before	during
vagabond	plus	exactly
of	the	around
as	near	without

How did you do? If we can use this short test to as an example of a learning period, then it may give you an idea of your memory's rhythm. General principles in memorization over a learning period is that people are more likely to remember information:

- If the information is encountered at <u>the beginning</u> or <u>the end</u> of a learning period.
- If the information is <u>repeated</u>.
- If the information has a <u>personal association</u>.
- If the information <u>stands out</u> from the rest.

In this particular test, it would be easiest to remember the first three to five words, the last two or three words, the word *the* (because of repetition) and the words *vagabond* (the only noun in the list) and *Disney*. In addition, we tend to remember our own specially associated groups of words, like the four basic mathematical operations: *plus*, *minus*, *multiply* and *divide* as well as words that for some personal reason are outstanding to us. It may or may not have been the case for you when you took the test, but as a general principle it is usually like this.

It is important to note which words were not remembered. As a general principle it would be anything that was not at the beginning or end of the learning period, that was not associated with other words and that was not in any way outstanding. In many cases, this means that all the information encountered in the middle section of the learning period is easily forgotten.

This is sometimes a problem if the students read a long, difficult text. If reading the text can be described as the whole learning period, then the students may have a good understanding of the beginning and the end of the text but may be missing information in the middle.

The point here is that understanding is not necessarily the same as recalling. The longer the learning period is, the more information will be lost. A solution to this problem is to create a learning environment in which both understanding and recalling can work at maximum capacity, which could easily be fixed by adding a few more breaks. By dividing a long learning period into multiple smaller periods, the students understanding will remain high and they will still be able to recall the information "in the middle" to some degree. After each learning period, the students should rest for about two to five minutes before continuing. After the break, the students should take a few seconds to recall what was learned in the last learning period as well as reviewing what is going to be learned in the upcoming learning period. This cycle of reviewing and previewing gives the students brain a target for the information they are going to encounter.

RECALL AFTER LEARNING

Once we have made it easier for our recollection to work during a learning period, we should optimize our recollection after the learning period. For this recollection the purpose is to let the information go from the short-term memory to the long-term memory and we can do that by using spaced repetition.

What surprises most people is that repetition immediately after the learning period has ended is not as effective as if we take a short break first. If we have been studying for one hour, the high point in our recall will be approximately ten minutes after the learning period, so this is the ideal time for our first review. The main reason for the first review is to take the information we have in our mind and make it more solid by using memory techniques.

If you manage to review after the first 10 minutes you may

find that the detailed information you have just obtained will not be lost but is maintained thanks to the mnemonics and mental images you have used. Typically, your first repetition should be 10 minutes after you learning period has ended, and the second repetition should be roughly 24 hours after that. This is because the decline in memory is extraordinarily high the first 24 hours, so even if you have used strong mental images, you are not out of the woods yet. After a week has passed it should be time to review the information for a third time. From here on out, you can judge by yourself how well your mnemonics works and should only be reviewed if you fear that your memory may be slipping. You can then review the information again after a month, six months and half a year, whenever you find it necessary.

Each review should not take up too much of your time. The first two reviews should be a complete review of your mental images and/or your Memory Palace. So, if you have created a Memory Palace you should imagine taking a walk through the location. After the first two repetitions you should be able to evaluate the memorization technique after the first week, by simply testing how much you are able to recall without completely reviewing your mental images or

Memory Palace. Any areas in which you are missing information you can decide by yourself whether the mental images you use are strong enough, or if it was simply a memory slip. If you for example used the same Memory Palace as I did in chapter 5 where we memorized the five largest oceans, then you should by now be able to judge if each of the five mental images works for you. If you can't recall them all, you should check the list of oceans and identify which of the mental images are not strong enough and either make them more memorable or completely change them.

THE TEACHERS ROLE IN REPETITION

As I mentioned at the beginning of this chapter, the students don't necessarily need to understand the theory but depending on the students it could be a good idea to teach them how to apply them anyways. If you ask the students to read a long text, tell them to stop after reading each sub chapter and review the information that they have just learned. It would be equivalent to you reading the previous section: RECALL AFTER LEARNING, and then review the information in your head before reading this section.

Before beginning on the next section, they should just read the headline, so they have an idea what they are going to learn. Pairing the students and make them explain it to each other could be a great way to do this as well.

Spaced repetition is a little easier for you to control, because you are usually the one deciding on a plan for each lecture, so whenever you have a lecture in which you are going to share important information, then you can plan a short repetition the next day and the next week. It can be challenging depending on how your schedule looks (in Denmark we only have one geography lecture per week), but if you can blend it in with other lectures then you may have a solution.

The challenge is to encourage the students to make the repetitions themselves. Even though they understand the value of spaced repetition, they are unlikely to take time aside to review their mental images or Memory Palace. One great thing I once saw a teacher do was to hang up a Mind Map in the classroom, containing all the topics covered in physics. That way the students could get an overview of the topics and recall some of the information from the keywords alone. One time I even heard a group of students trying to recall the principles of radioactive half-life in one of their breaks.

Exercises

When most people think of memory exercises, they think about a game they can play on their phone. While such games are great at exercising specific skillsets, they are not enough to improve memorization. In this chapter, you will find seven simple exercises to improve memory and concentration. Some of them are already included in the previous chapters, but for your convenience they are repeated here.

- Working Memory with Math
- Listen and Recall
- Simple Objects – Multiple Uses!
- The Metronome-Clapping Exercise
- The Short-Term Memory Tester
- Four Details Observation
- What Color is a Subject?

WORKING MEMORY WITH MATH

We can use numeracy to boost our working memory. It doesn't include any memory techniques, but it is more like a dumbbell to strengthen the concentration and logical thinking.

Start out by giving the students a three-digit number. Then then tell them to add 3 to that number 3 times. Afterwards tell them to subtract 7 from that new number 7 times. For example, starting out with the number 689 it would look like this:

689 + 3 + 3 + 3 = 698

698 - 7 - 7 - 7 - 7 - 7 - 7 – 7 = 649

It is crucial that the students does not write anything down. The point of the exercise is not to practice math but to strengthen the working memory because of the amount of detail they need to hold in their mind to complete the task. The amount of digits you use as the initial number is of course depending on the students and you are not limited to using 3 and 7. A variation could be to pair the students and let them challenge each other's by determining the numbers using dices.

LISTEN AND RECALL

In the Danish language we have two different words for listening: *lytte* and *høre efter*. The difference is that *høre efter* means that you are actively focusing on what is being said, while *lytte* simply means that you are aware that something is being said but you don't really pay attention to it.

Everyone who have ever taught a class of kids can identify the latter. Often students ignore what the teacher says and afterwards comes to the teacher for help about something they would have known if they had paid attention two minutes earlier. This happens for both engaging teachers as well as boring teachers. The good news is that the art of *høre efter* can actually be practiced with one simply habit.

When someone is talking to you about something important, you have to repeat every word they are saying silently in your head.

This simple habit does not only boost your social skills, it also trains you brain to focus on what people are telling you and remember they say. You will automatically boost your cognitive function and remember more by doing this.

SIMPLE OBJECTS – MULTIPLE USES!

This exercise can be really fun when teaching younger students. Fill a sack with various items, like a mug, spoon, sock, etc. Divide the students into small groups and let each group randomly select an item. Set a timer to three or five minutes and let the students brainstorm all the possible uses this item have.

In chapter 4 I gave you a similar exercise, where you had to find creative uses for a sock. This exercise strengthens the students' creativity so they easily can create memorable mental images.

THE METRONOME-CLAPPING EXERCISE

A few years back I read about this exercise to improve concentration, which I found absurd to begin with, but ended up practicing ever since. I have even used in the beginning of some lectures when I needed the student's full attention.

You put on a metronome at a slow speed and then tell the students to clap on each click.

This does not help the students improve their memory but instead gives an enhanced focus for some time. A metronome generator can easily be found on Google if you search for *metronome*. I always lower the BPM (Beat Per Minute) to around 40, which means that there will be a beat once each 1½ second, forcing the students to focus on the beat instead of automatically clap their hands every second as they would with 60 BPM.

THE SHORT-TERM MEMORY TESTER

Find a memory game – if possible one with detailed images. Remove all duplicates so you only have one of each card. The recommended number of cards is between 25 and 49.

Show two cards to the students. After an agreed amount of time shuffle the cards together with the others and place them on a table with the picture side up. The task for the students is to identify the cards which they were shown before. As the game progresses, more and more cards will be shown to the students.

This exercise challenges the students short term memory, as they have to instantly recall the cards which they have just been shown. As the students becomes familiar with creating mental images, this game can be used to evaluate how well they understand the concepts.

FOUR DETAILS OBSERVATION

The next time you meet someone else, note four details about this person so you are able to visualize him or her later. It could be the clothes they are wearing, the way their hair look, some special gestures in their face or an animal they remind you of. You can benefit from this small exercise in multiple ways.

For one thing, it is a great social skill to be observant of others around you. Ever heard about the phrase "To be interesting you have to be interested"? Being interesting is actually an attractive trait for most women, which by the way is a great selling point if you have a lot of boys in the classroom.

The other thing, and this is of course why I included it in this book, is that it helps your visualization skills. If you are in the habit of noticing details about someone or something, then you are able to imagine much more detailed mental images. It could of course also be useful to use this exercise with cars, buildings or animals to help you further.

WHAT COLOR IS A SUBJECT?

This is a question that creates an informal discussion between the students. It gives them awareness of association, because it makes the students think about other ways of looking at the subject than the traditional way. Most students agree that biology is green, because they associate the subject with plants, but there can come some interesting responses from some students. For example: some students think history is gray like a colorless photography and some think it is brownish because of the color of old paper.

Afterword

I hope that you have enjoyed reading this book and that you now have a greater insight in the process of learning. Ideally you now understand how your brain works and which evolutionary advantages you can use to store even complex information in your long-term memory. When you use the techniques taught in this book, the ability of your brain can easily bypass the size of even the best filing systems in the world. Remember that this is the same techniques used by memory champions, like Dominic O'Brien.

If the content in this book have made you interested in this area of self-exploration and improvement, you are well advised to practice and apply the different memorization techniques in your day-to-day life as well as your teaching methods. I have given examples to show you how I use memorization to remember grammar, vocabulary and numbers, but you must develop your own systems and so must your students. What makes sense to me may not make sense to you and likewise, what makes sense to you may not make sense to me. The importance is not for it to make sense to others than yourself, the importance is that you can use it to remember. Try not to overdo it by putting it all into practice in one go. A small dose of practice every day is much better than an overload of activities followed by frustration. After all, Rome was not built overnight.

Apart from the basic principle of using memorization techniques there is one particular aspect of this book that I would like you to think about, and that is the power of imagination. It should by now be clear to you that the development of memory skills not only gives you the advantage of being able to store more information in your brain than you used to but also celebrates the use of imagination and creativity in the learning process. Imagination is the tool children use when they learn and few can argue against children being the best learners. It makes everything in the world easier to understand, whether it is within the arts, languages or science. Information is everywhere and it is worth spending time on a tool that makes it accessible and memorable.

Bibliography

Buzan, Tony. *Italian: Learning meets Mind Mapping.* Collins (2008)

Buzan, Tony. *Use Your Memory.* Guild Publishing (1986)

Dingman, Marc. *Your Brain Explained: What Neuroscience Reveals About Your Brain and its Quirks.* Mobius (2019)

Dweck, Carol. *Mindset: The New Psychology of Success.* Ballantine Books (2007)

Edwards, Vanessa Van. *Captivate: The Science of Succeeding with People.* Portfolio Penguin (2017)

Ferriss, Tim. *The 4-Hour Chef: The Simple Path to Cooking Like a Pro, Learning Anything, and Living the Good Life.* Amazon Publishing (2012)

Imsen, Gunn. *Elevens Verden: Indføring i Pædagogisk Psykologi, 4th Edition.* Gyldendal (2006)

Khoo, Adam. *I Am Gifted, So Are You!* Marshall Cavendish (2014)

Levi, Jonathan. *Become a SuperLearner: Learn Speed Reading & Boost Memory.* Udemy: https://www.udemy.com/course/become-a-superlearner-2-speed-reading-memory-accelerated-learning/

Levi, Jonathan. *The Only Skill That Matters: The Proven Methodology to Read Faster, Remember More, and Become a SuperLearner.* Lioncrest Publishing (2019)

Metivier, Anthony. *How to Learn and Memorize the Vocabulary of Any Language.* Udemy: https://www.udemy.com/course/language-learning-online-magnetic-memory/

Metivier, Anthony. *The Ultimate Language Learning Secret (Magnetic Memory Series).* Createspace Independent Pub (2014)

Miller, George A. Psychological Review (1956)

O'Brien, Dominic. *How to Develop Perfect Memory.* Pavilion Books (1993)

O'Brien, Dominic. *Quantum Memory Power.* Simon Schuster Audio/Nightingale-Conant (2001)

Robinson, Ken. *Out of Our Minds: The Power of Being Creative, 3rd Edition.* Capstone (2017)

Robinson, Ken. *The Element: How Finding Your Passion Changes Everything.* Viking Books (2009)

Waitzkin, Josh. *The Art of Learning: An Inner Journey to Optimal Performance.* Free Press (2007)

Index